MY VALUE ISN'T NEGOTIABLE

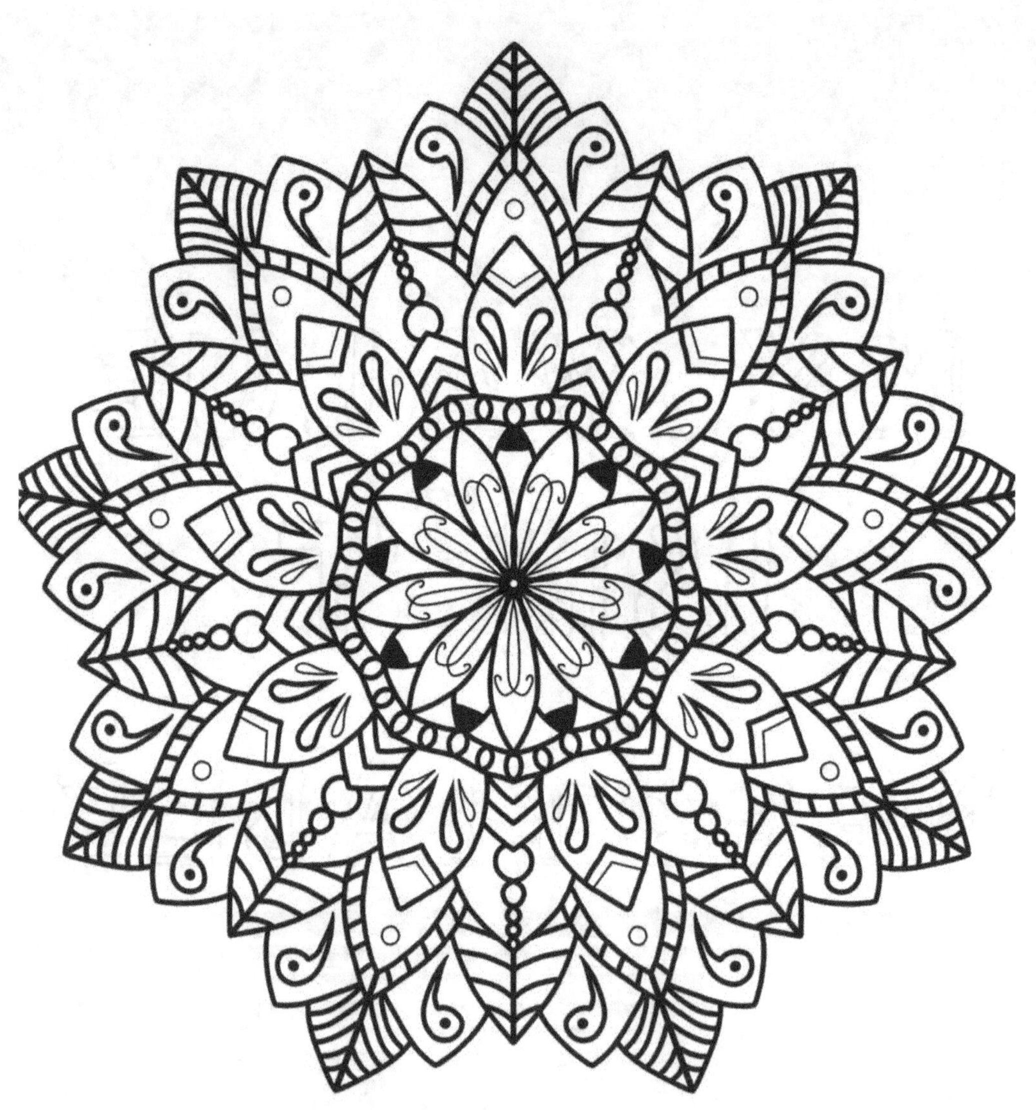

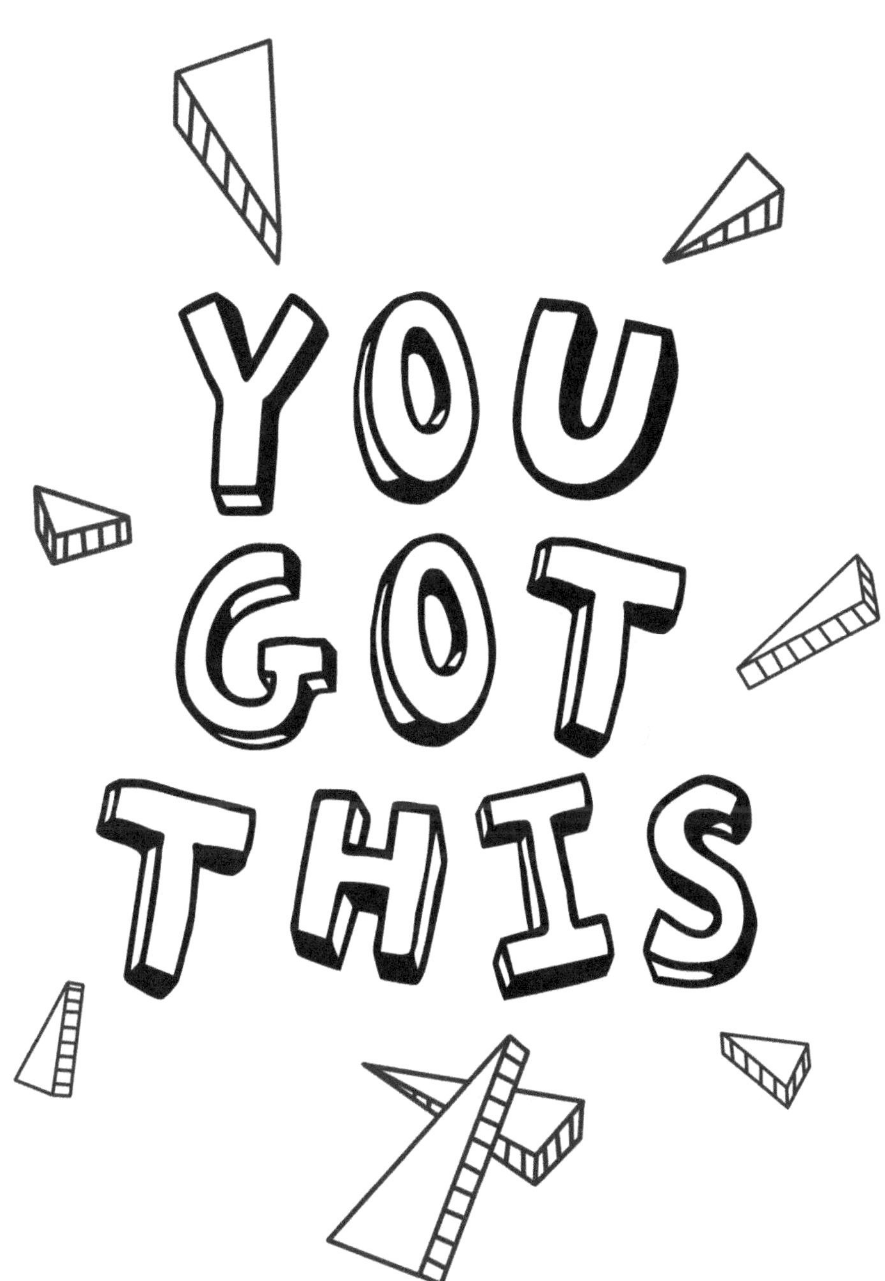
YOU
GOT
THIS

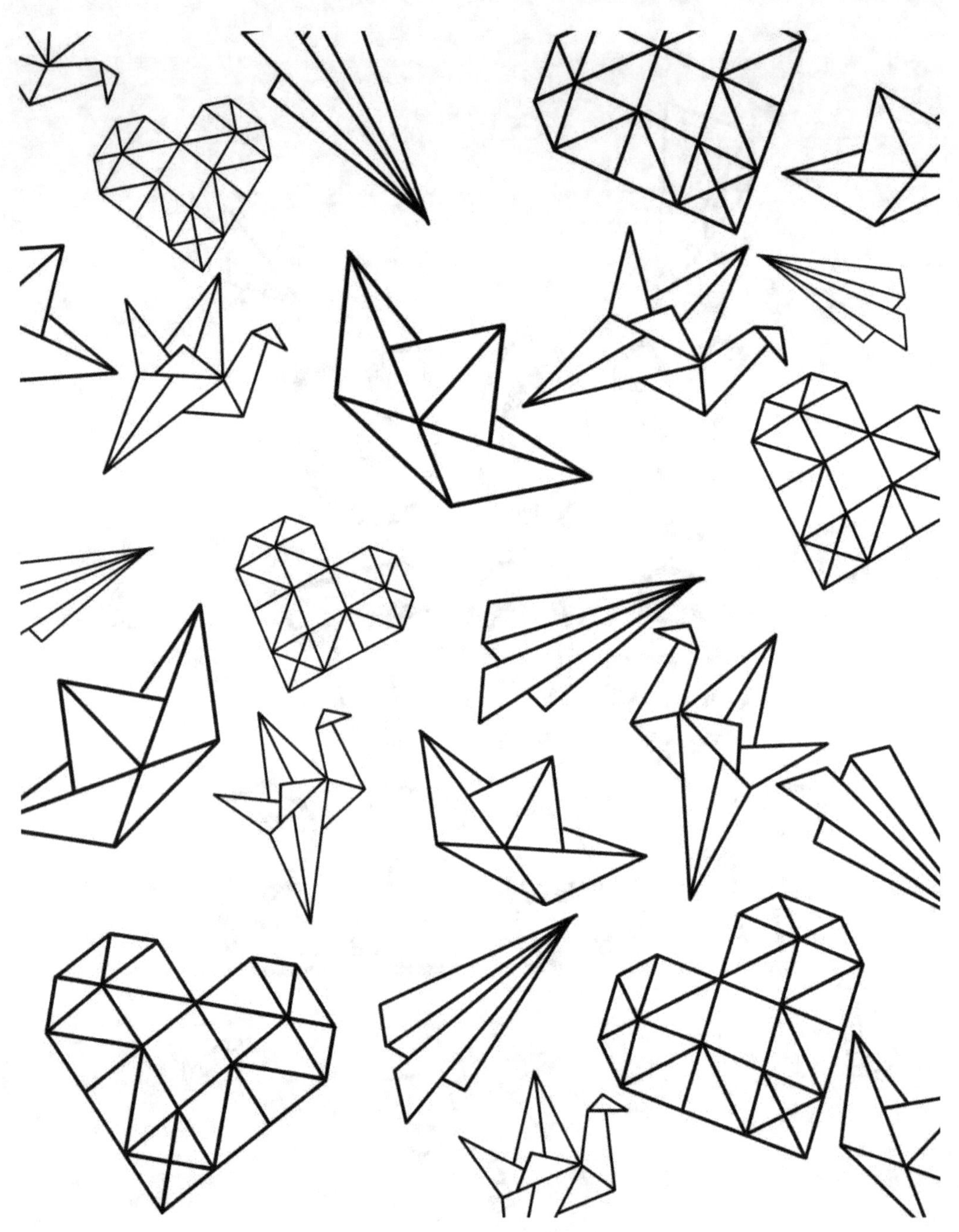

FAITHFUL

FLAWLESS

FIERCE

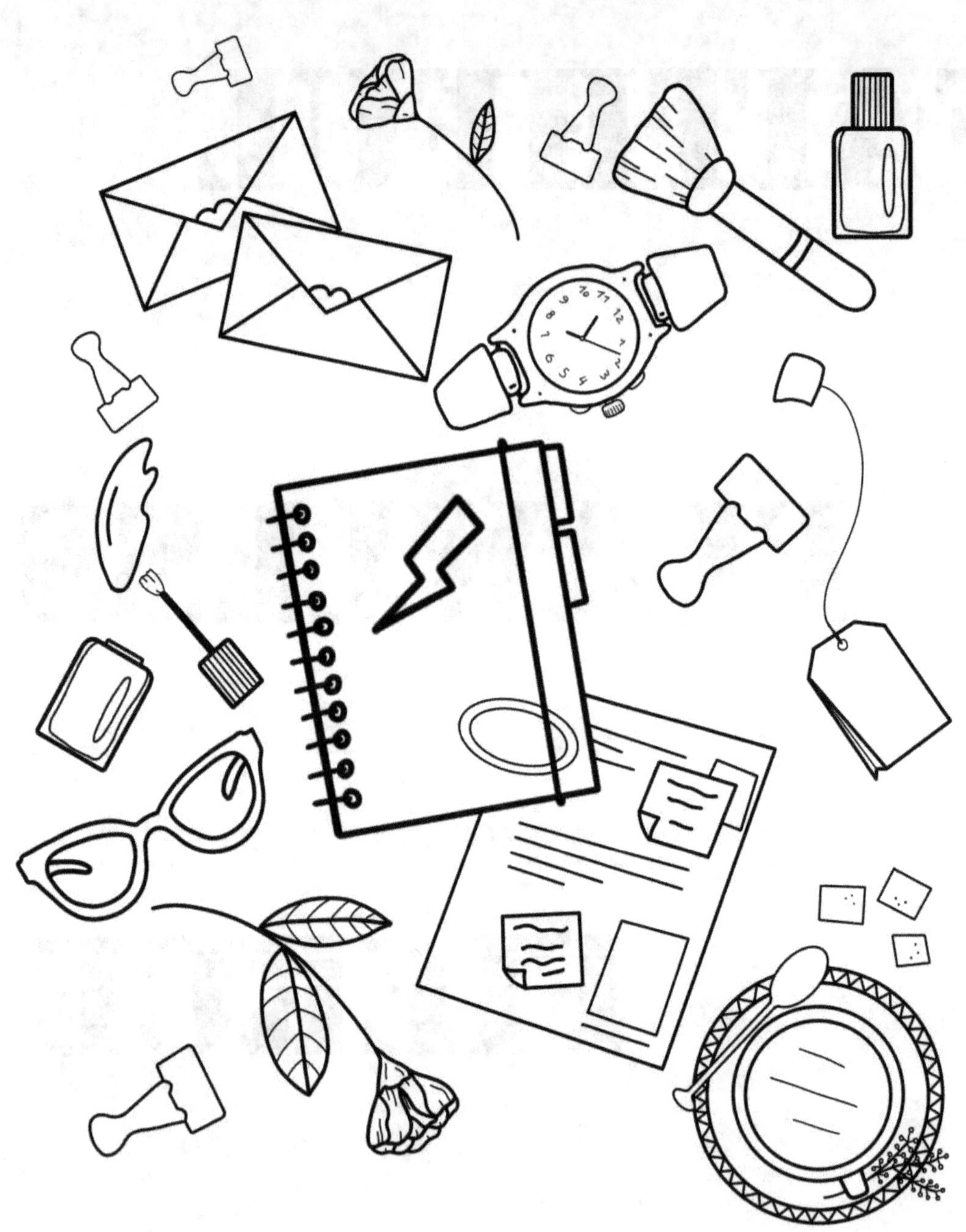

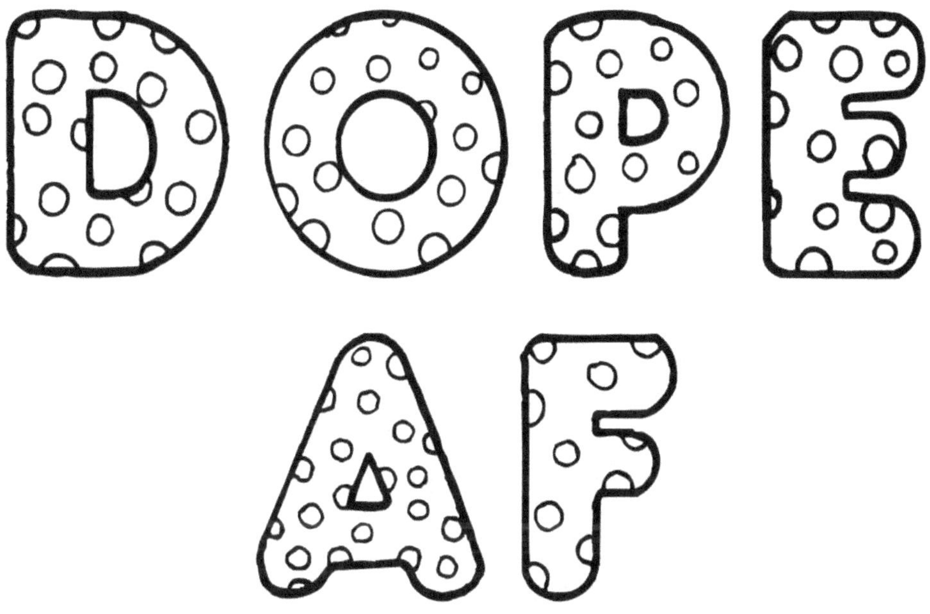
DOPE
AF

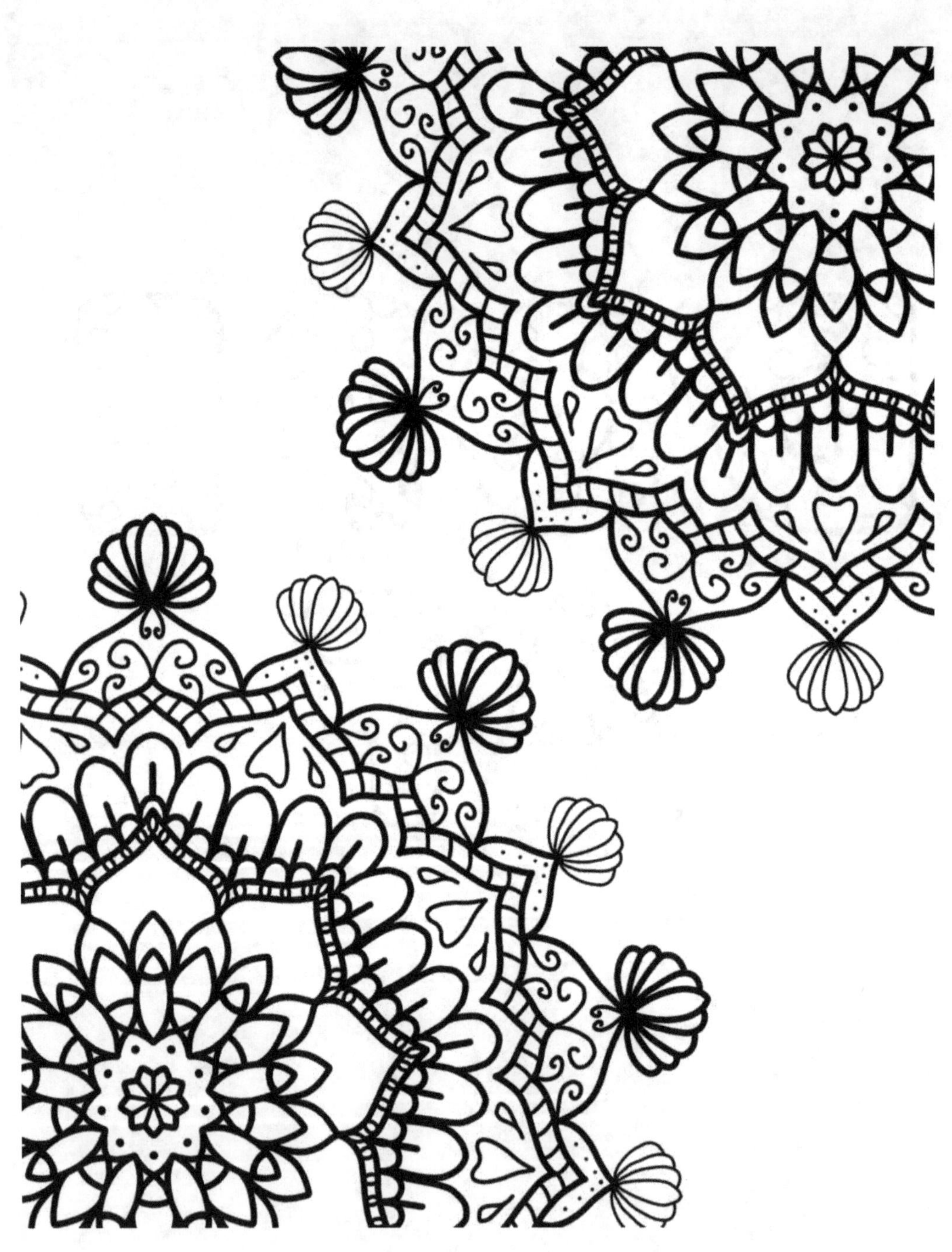

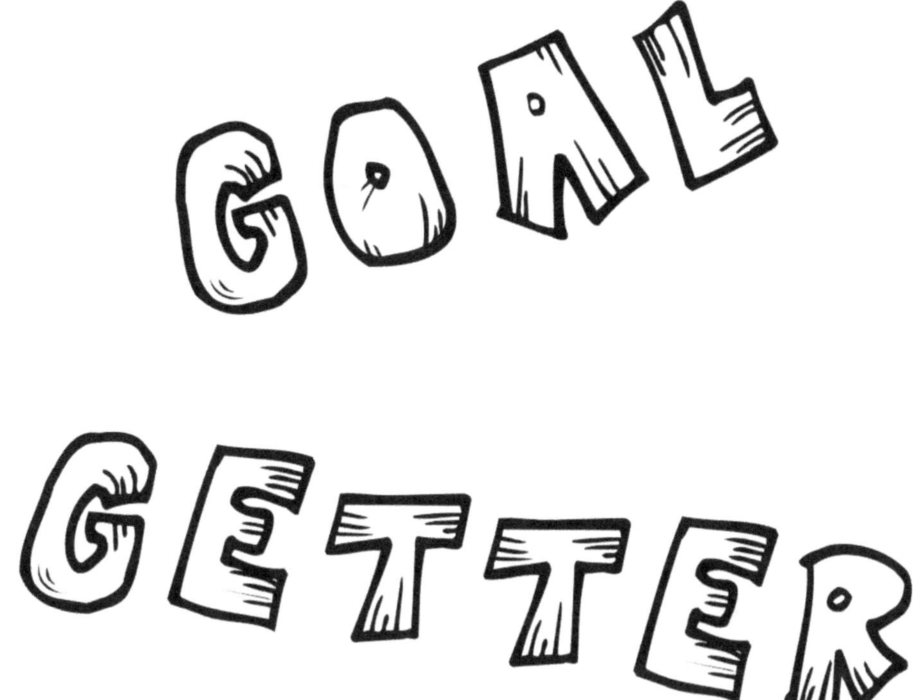
GOAL
GETTER

FAITH OVER FEAR

GIRLS
RULE

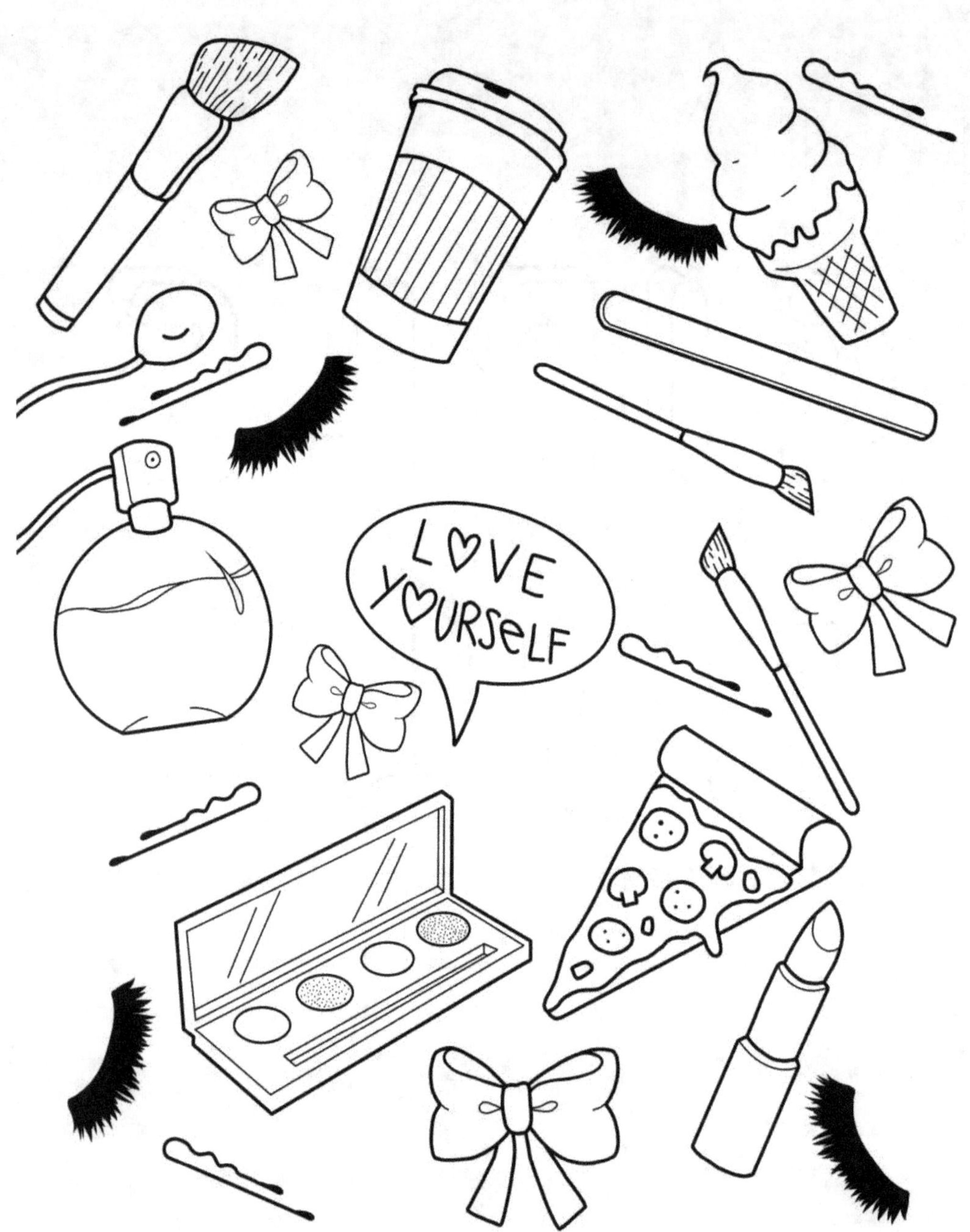
LOVE
YOURSELF

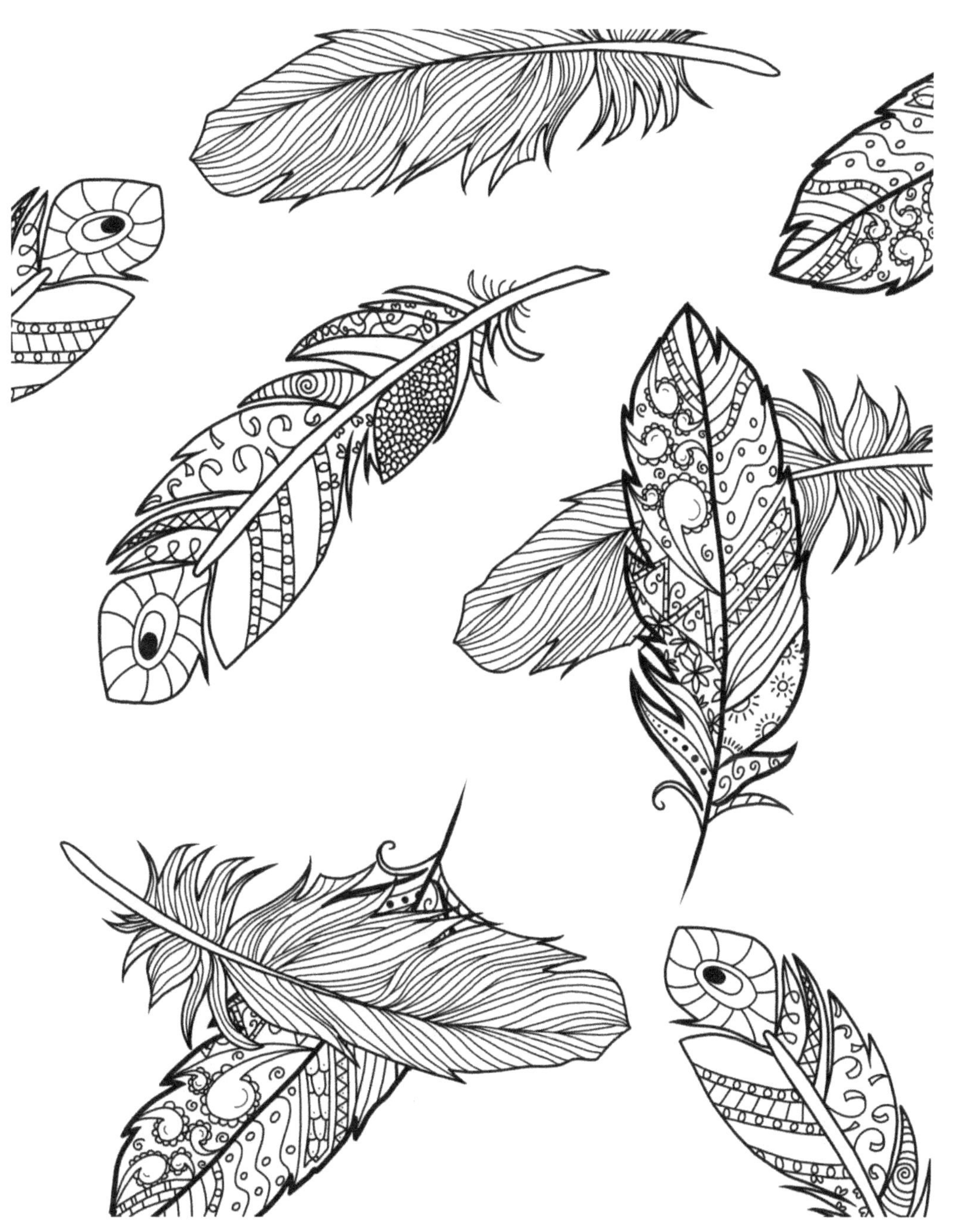

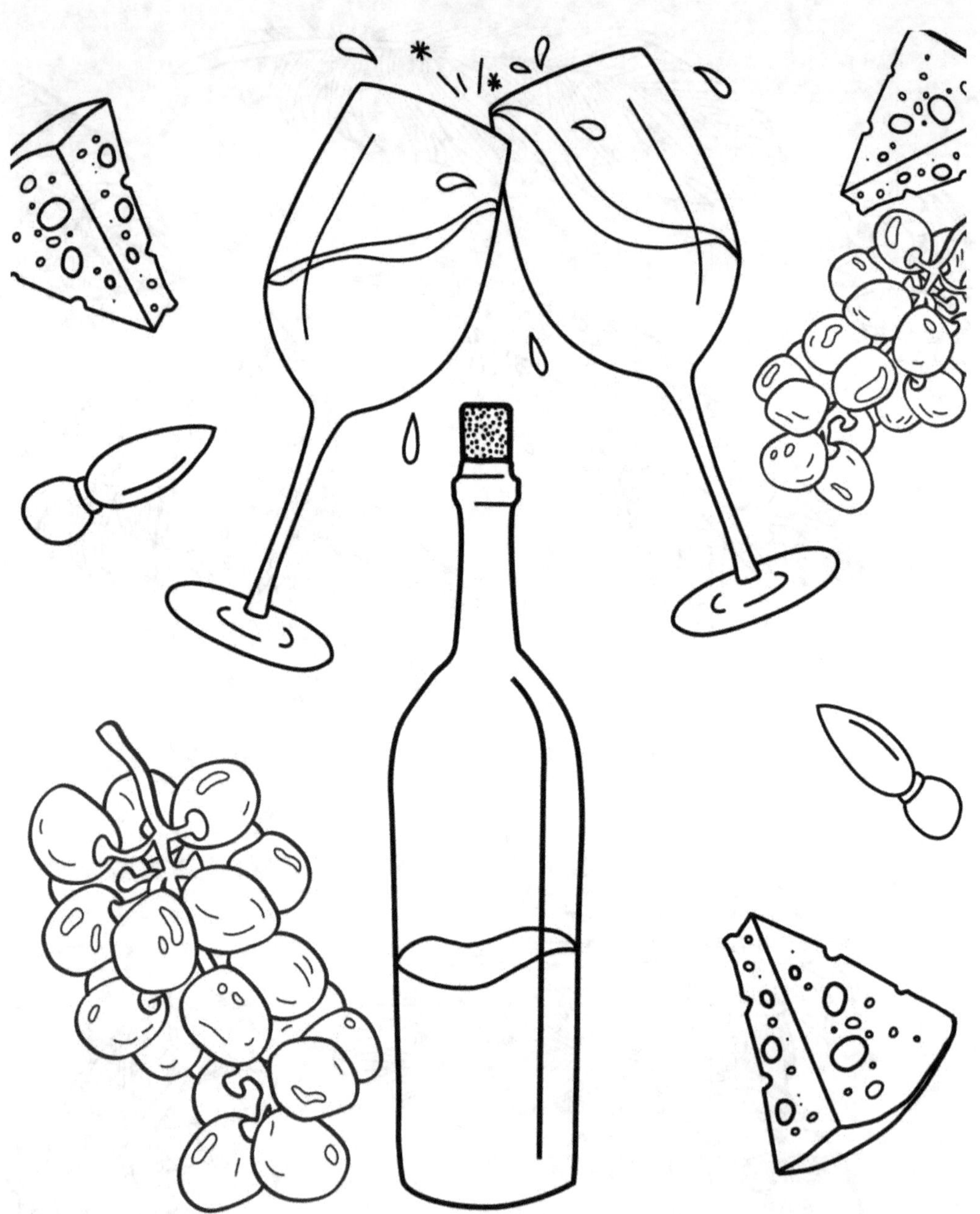

BOSS CHICK

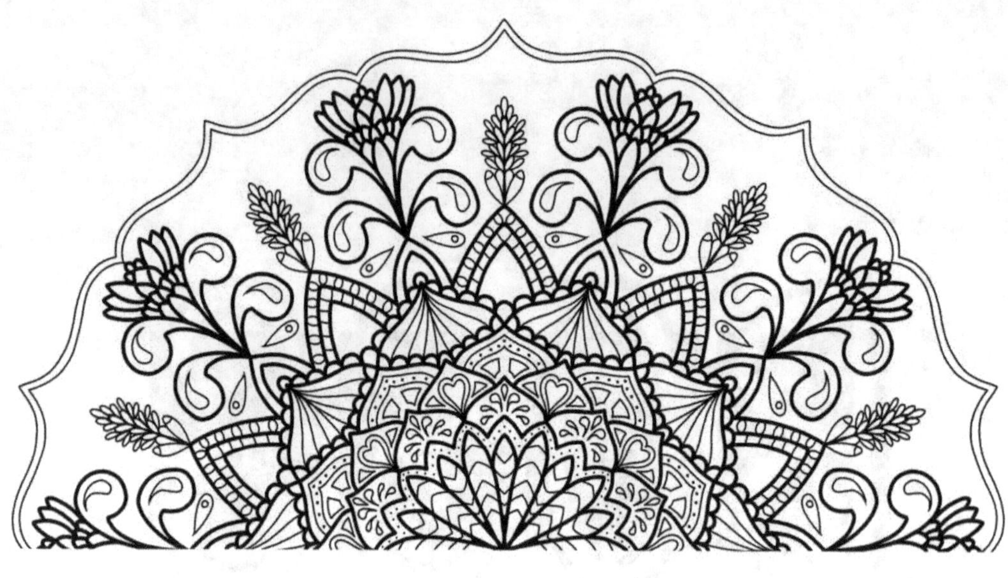

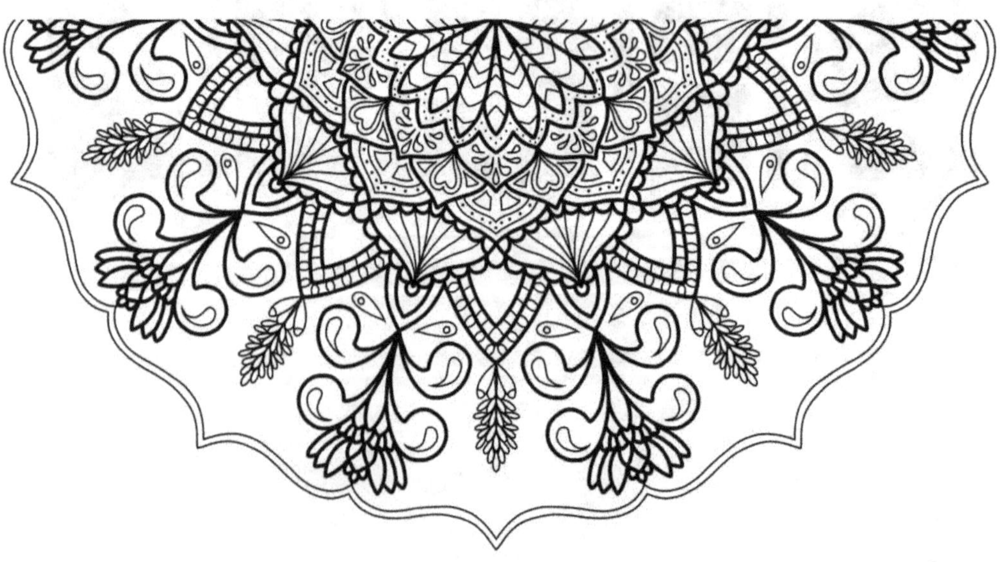

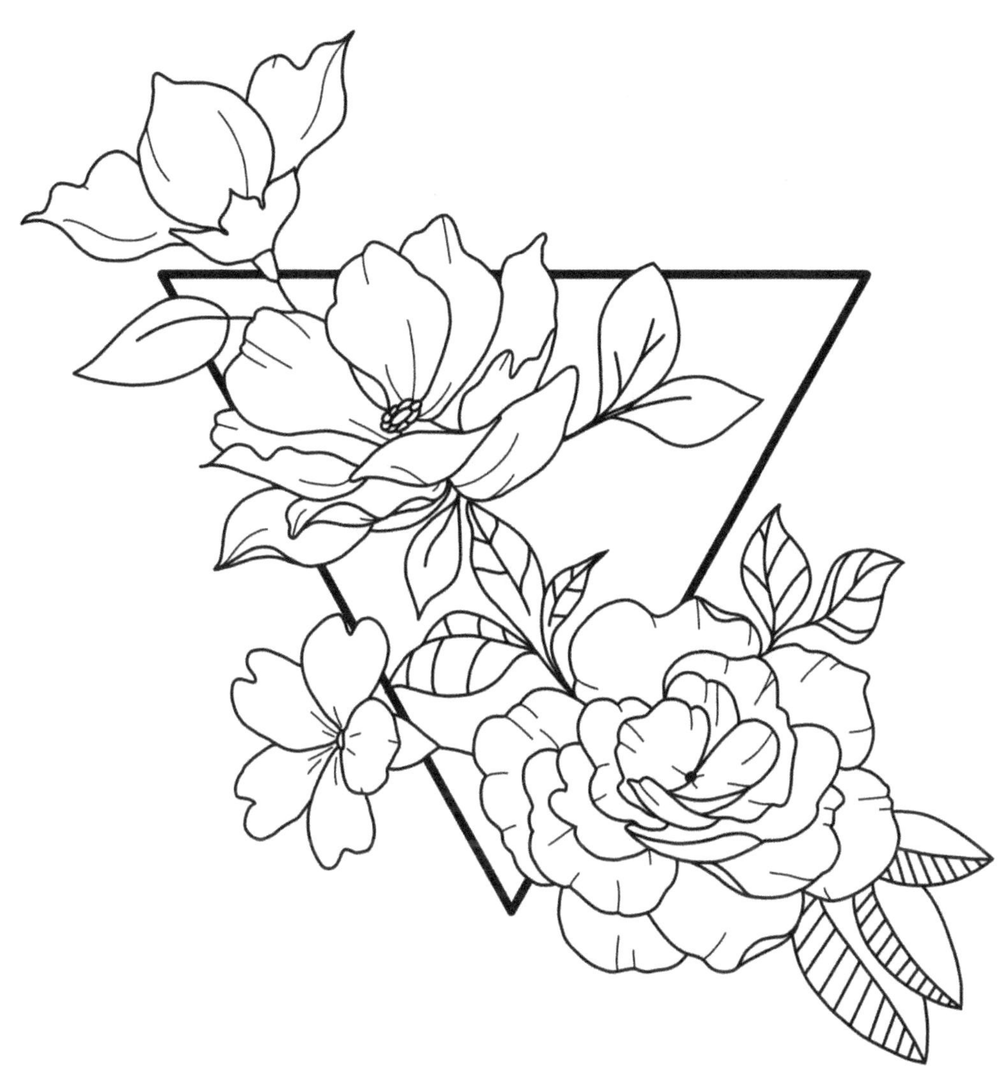

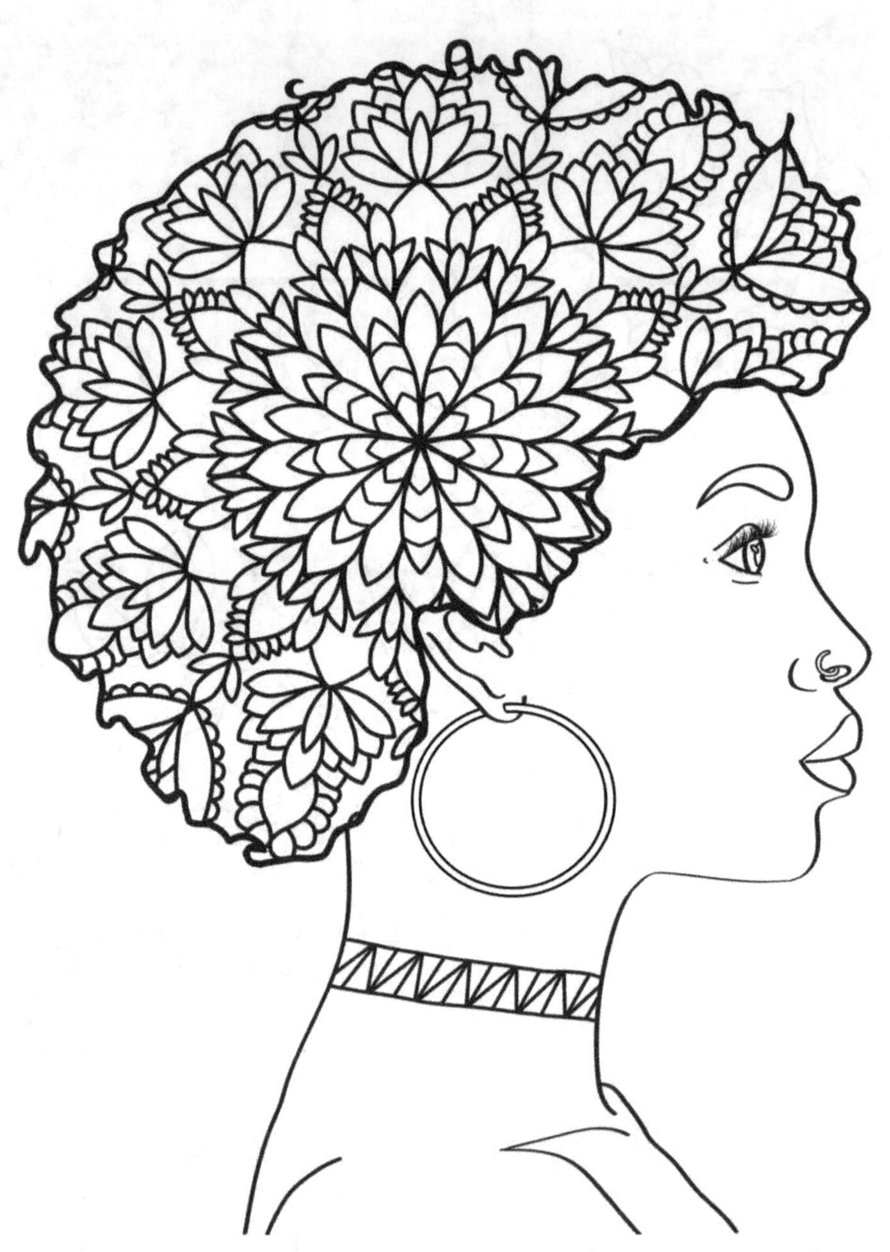

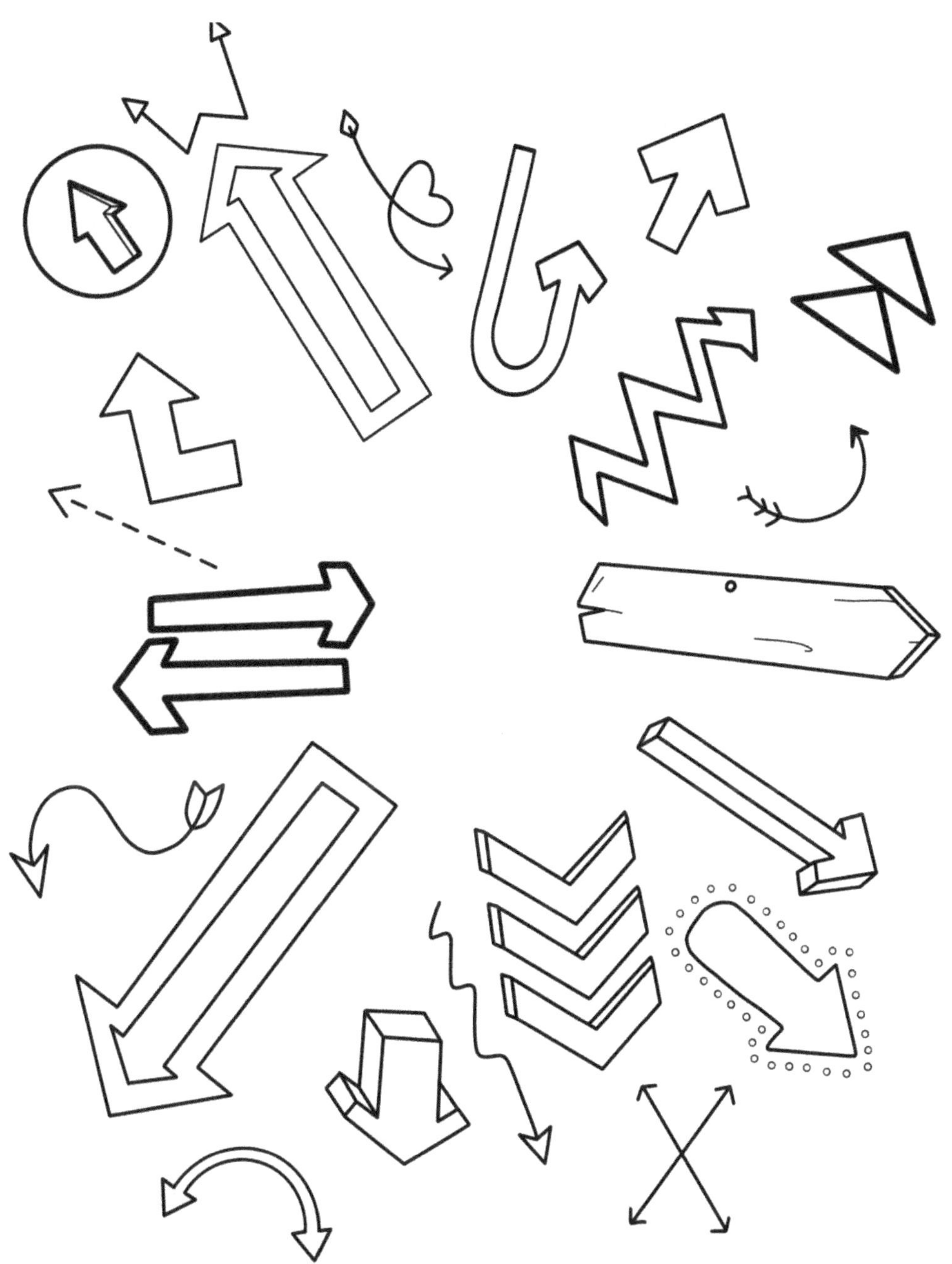

HAPPINESS
IS
A
CHOICE

MOM
MOM

DON'T GET MAD

GET DISTANT

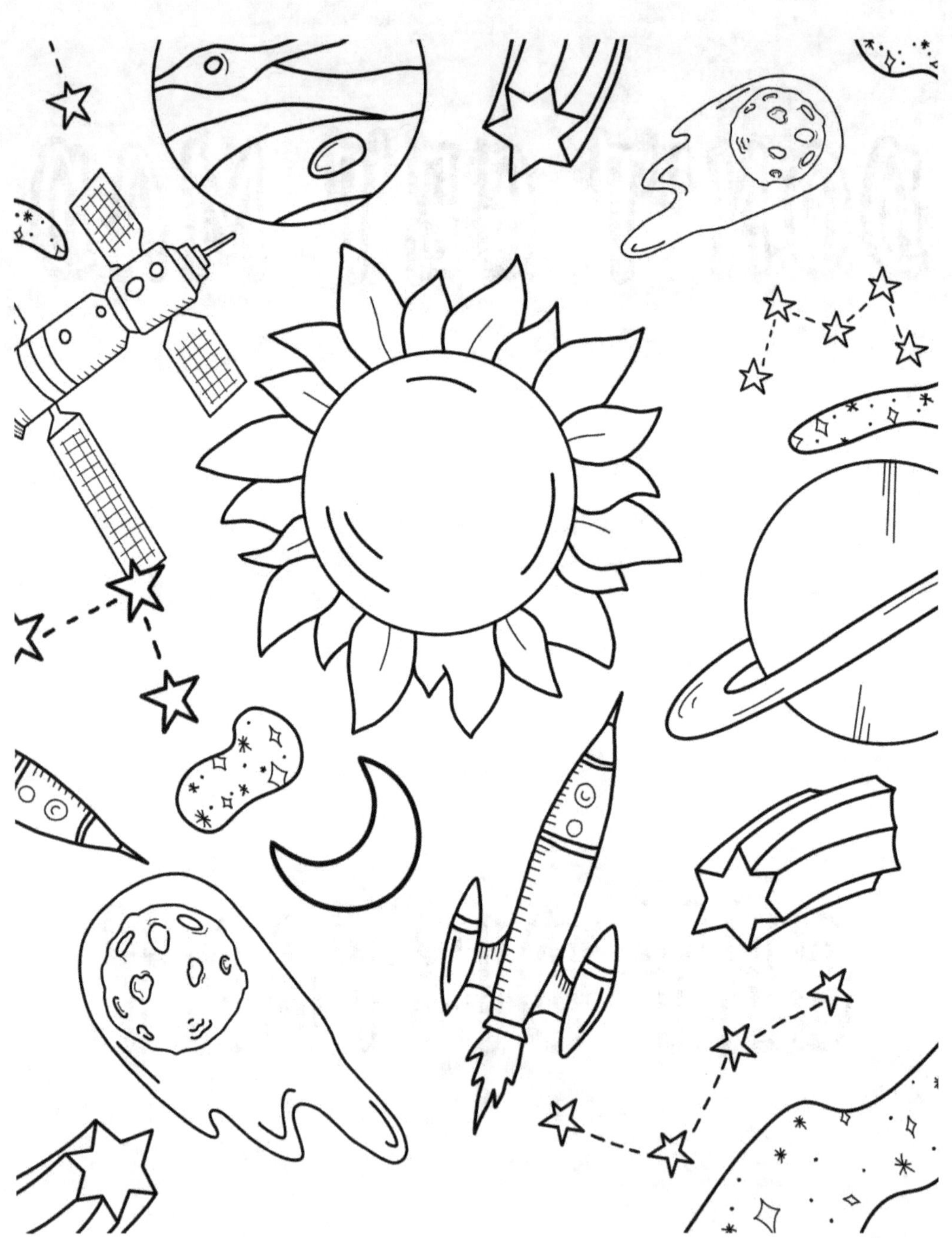

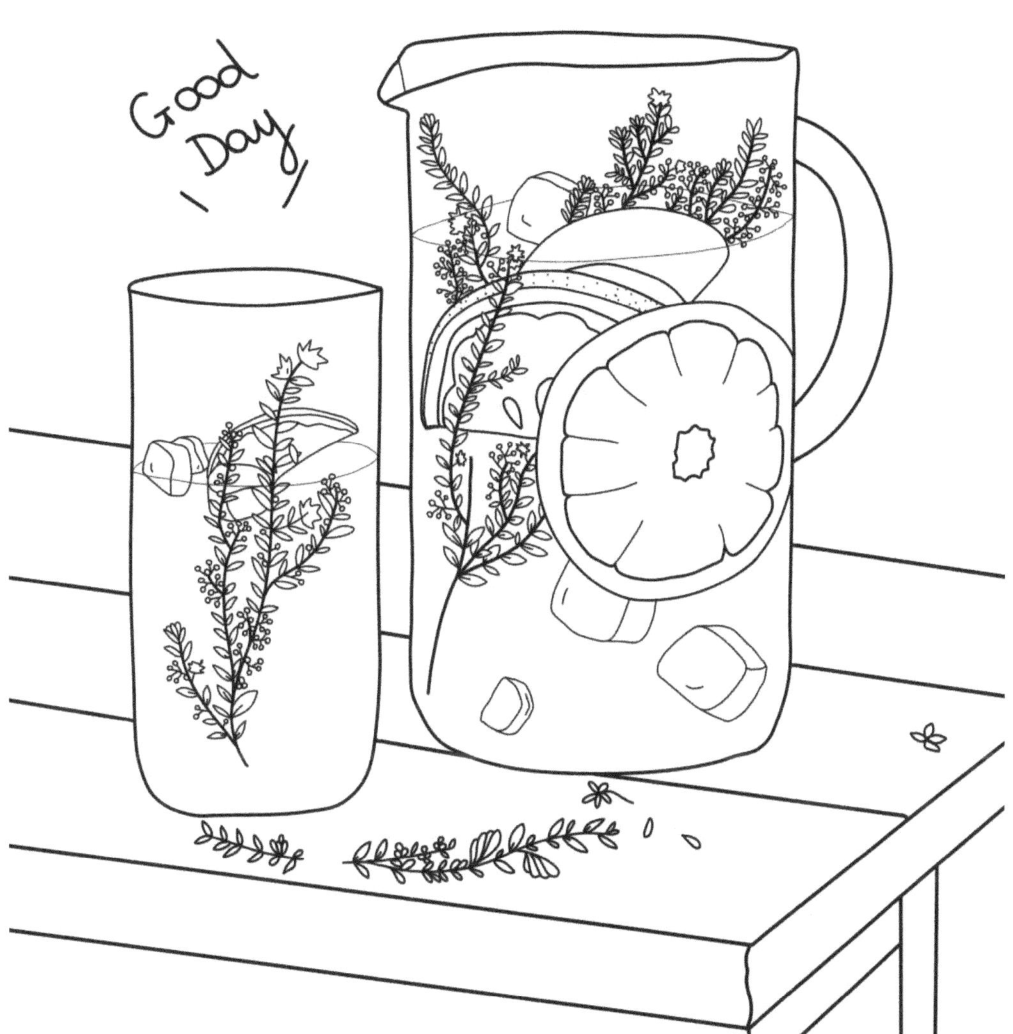
Good
Day

DOPE

WOMEN

ROCK

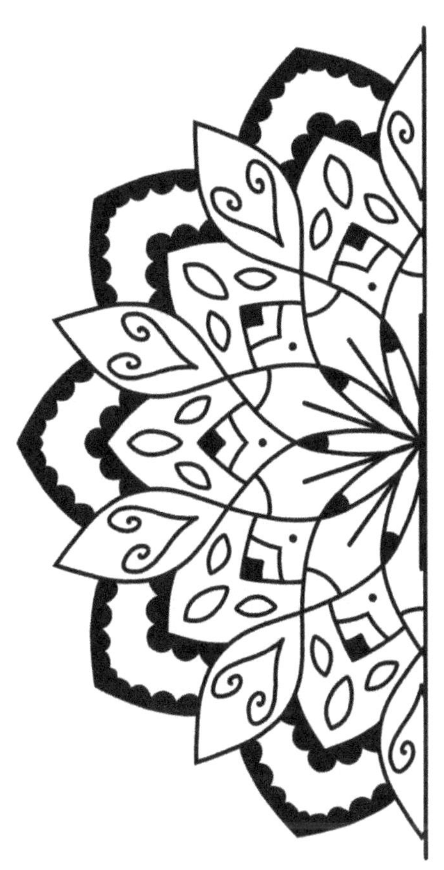
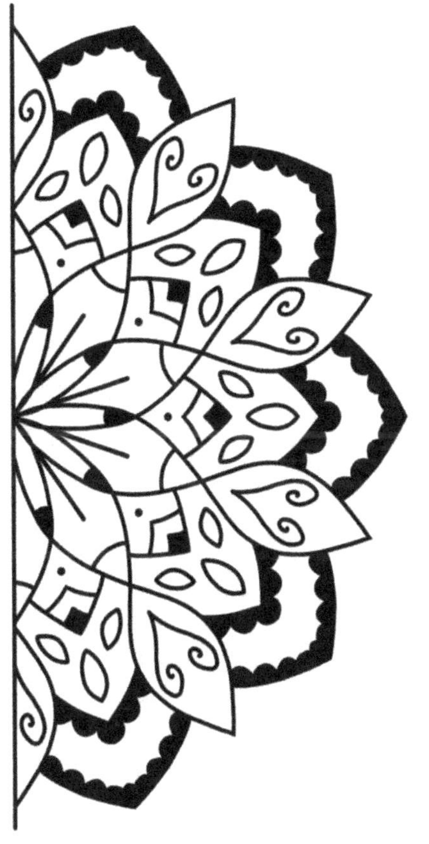

CHIN UP QUEEN

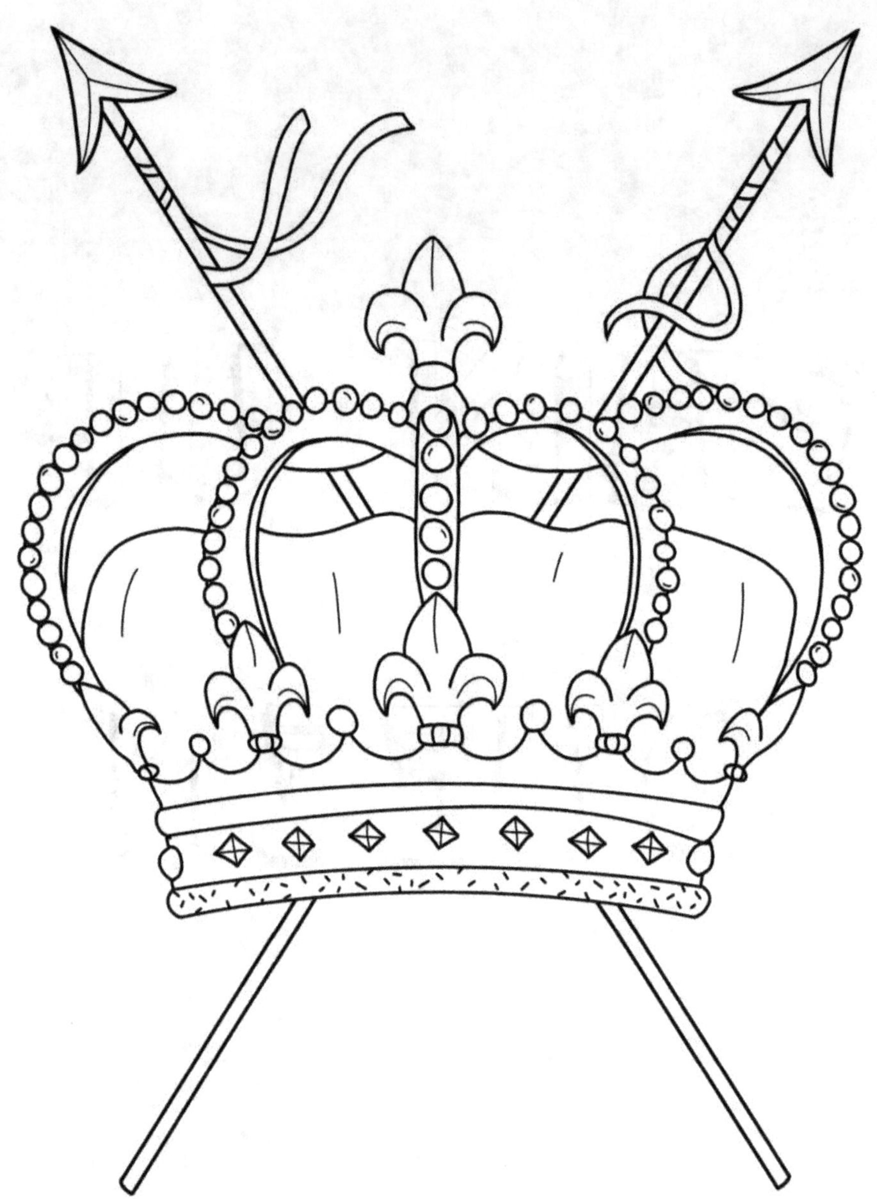

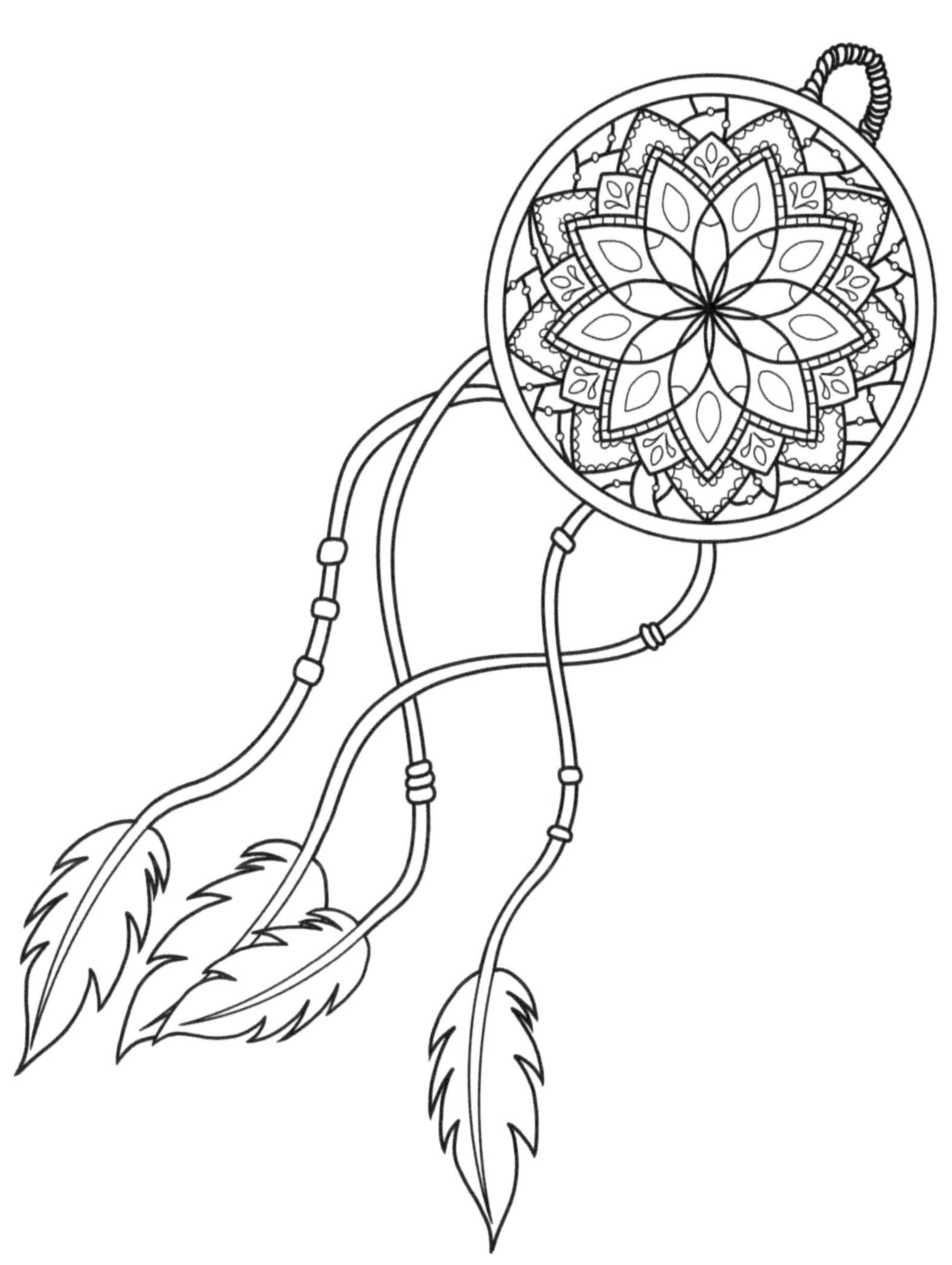

BE AWAKEN

BY YOUR

PASSION

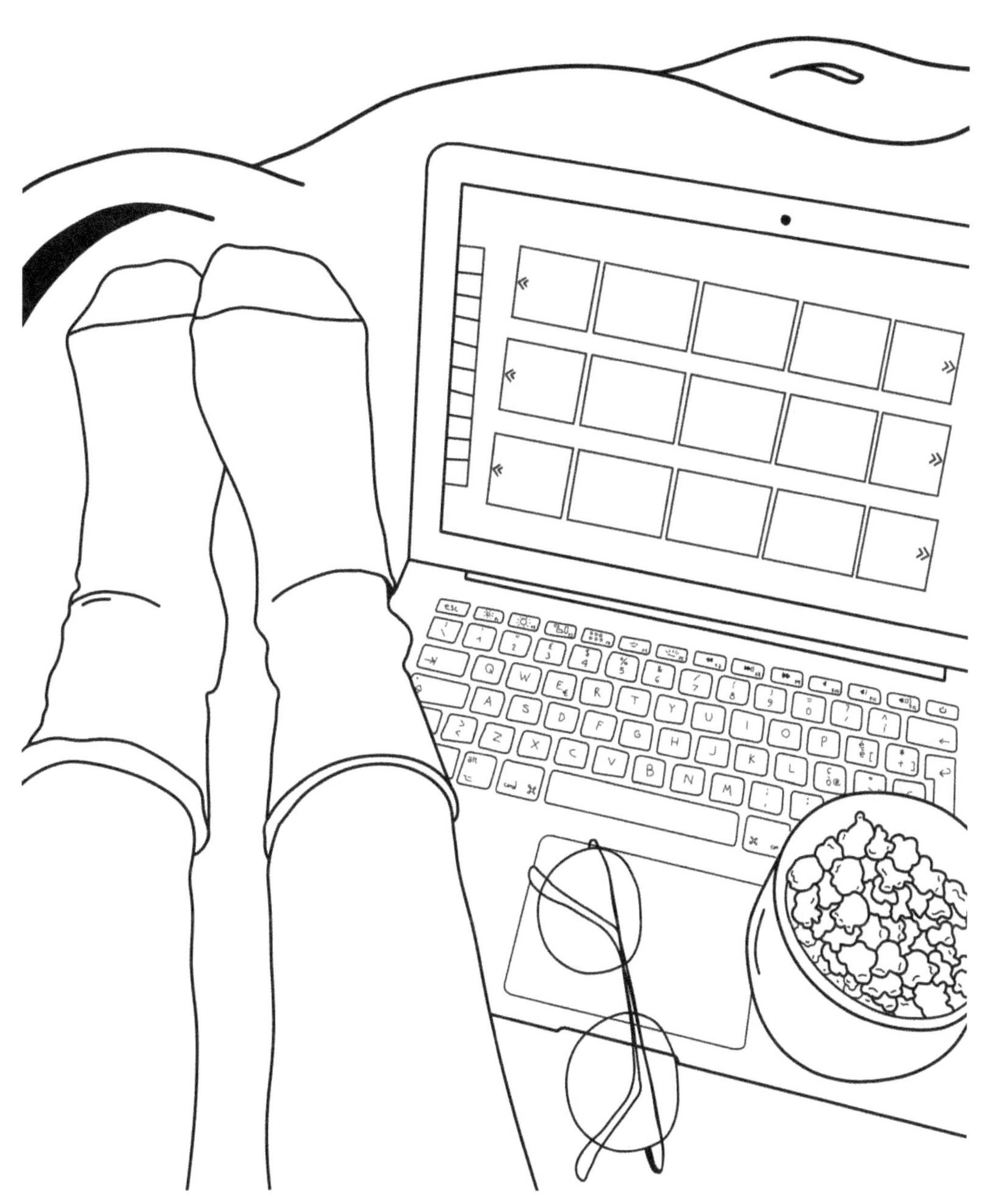

THIS JOURNEY IS PERSONAL

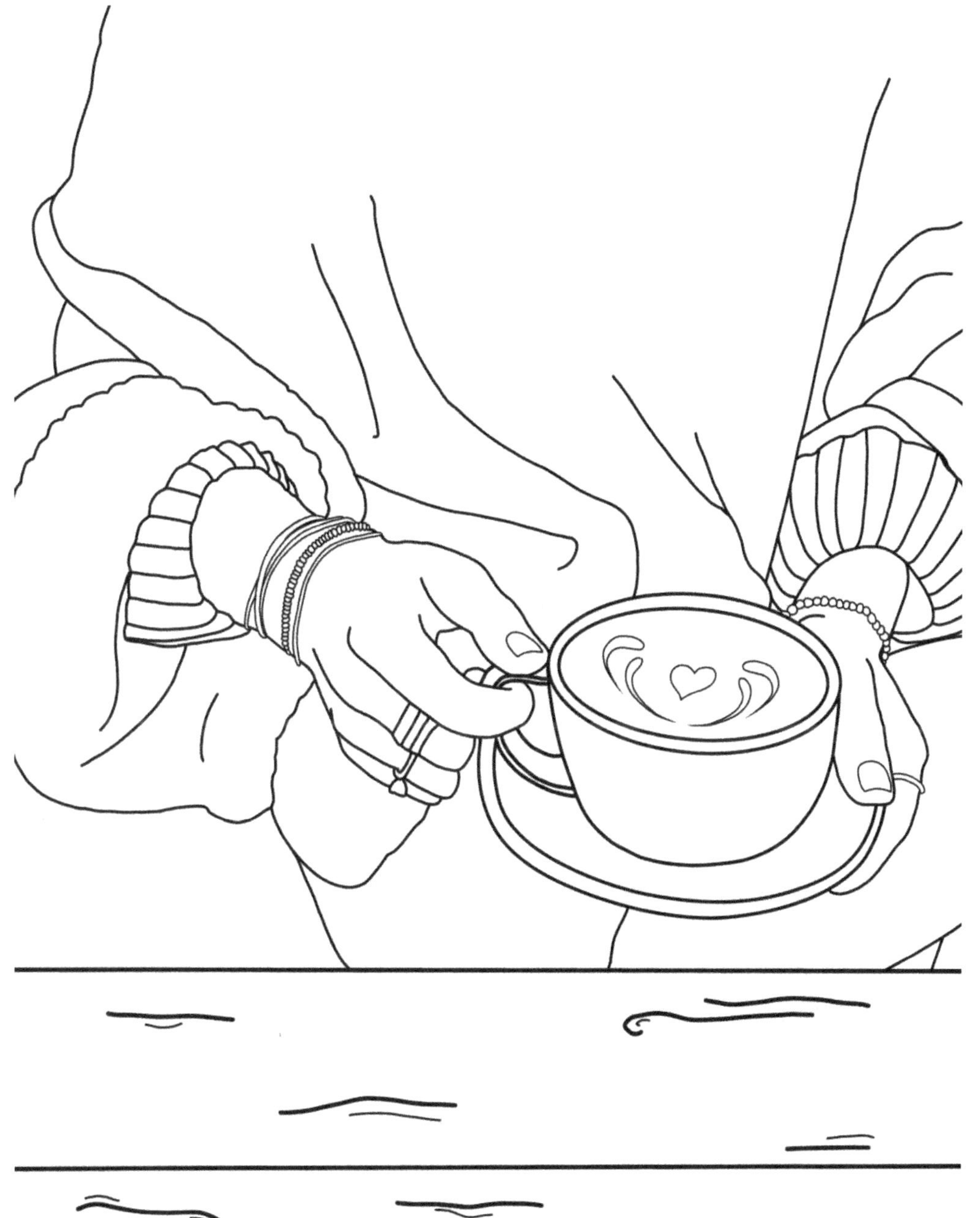

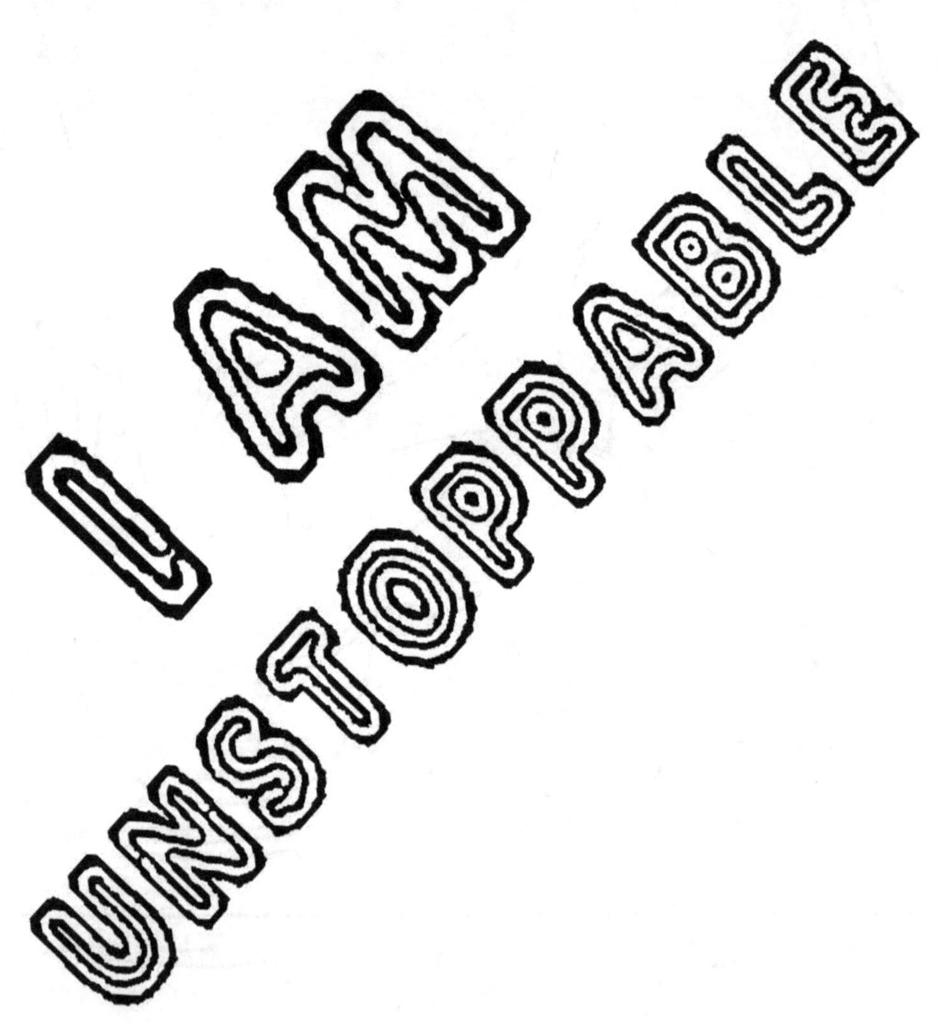
I AM
UNSTOPPABLE

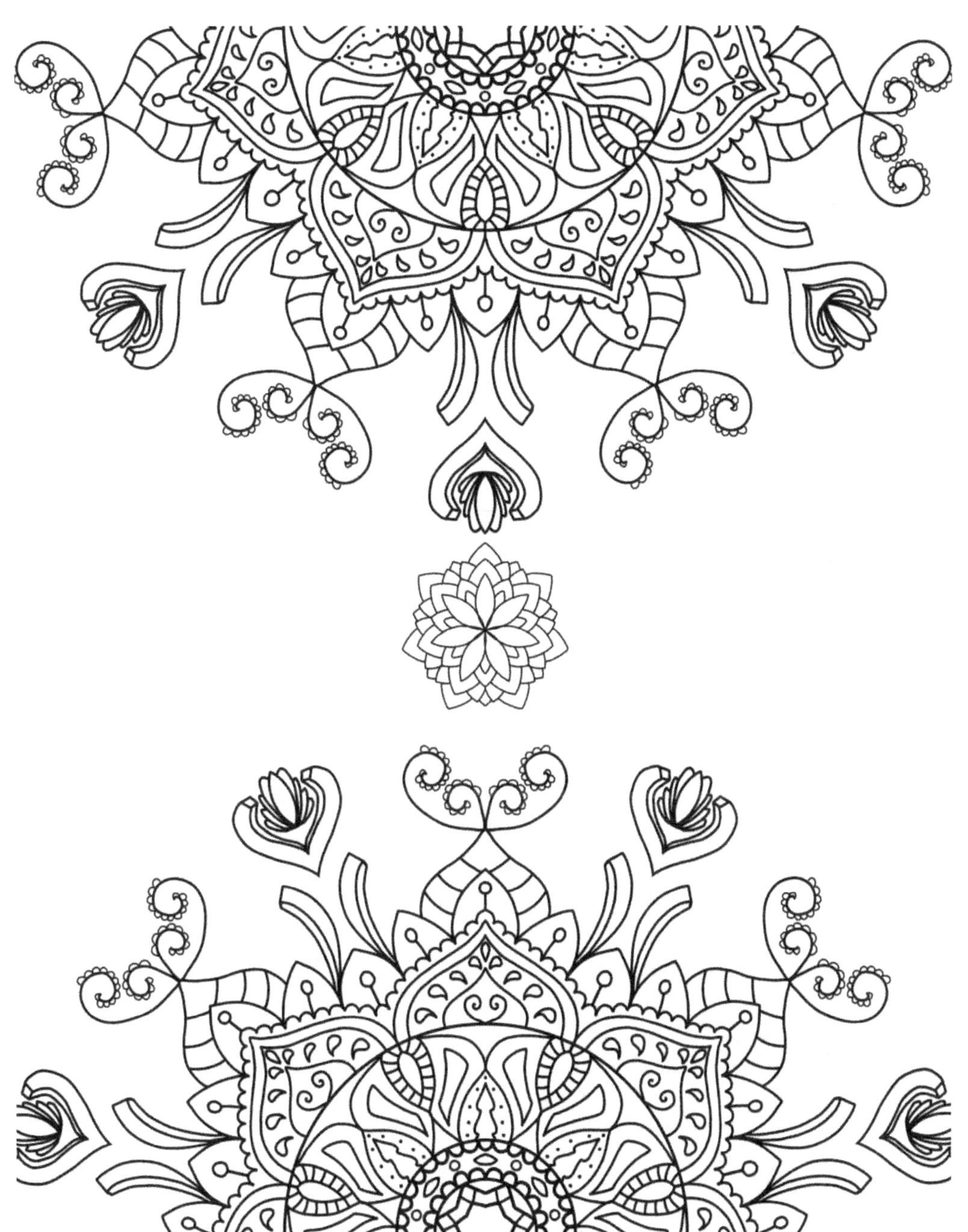

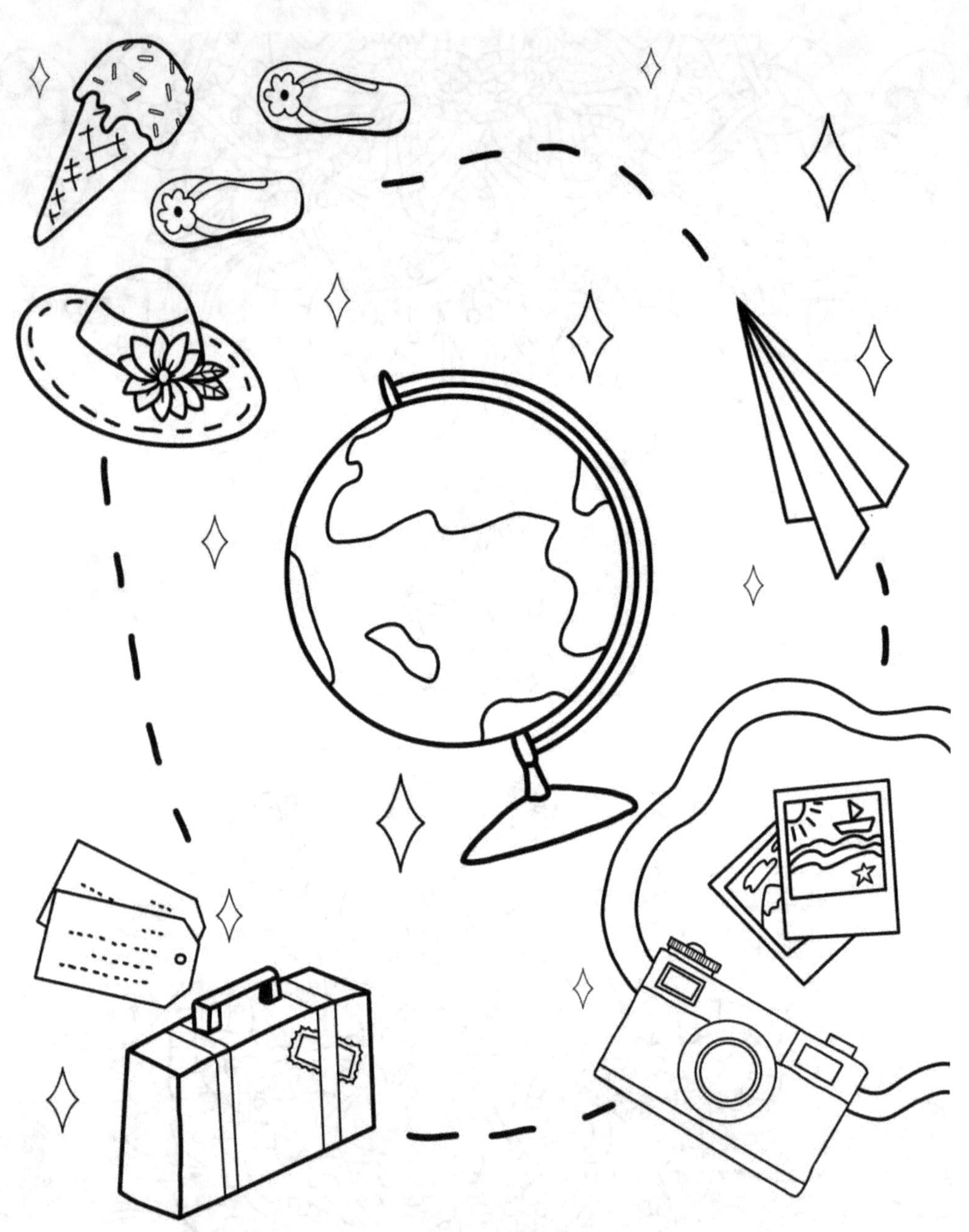

IMAGINE.
ACHIEVE.
BELIEVE.

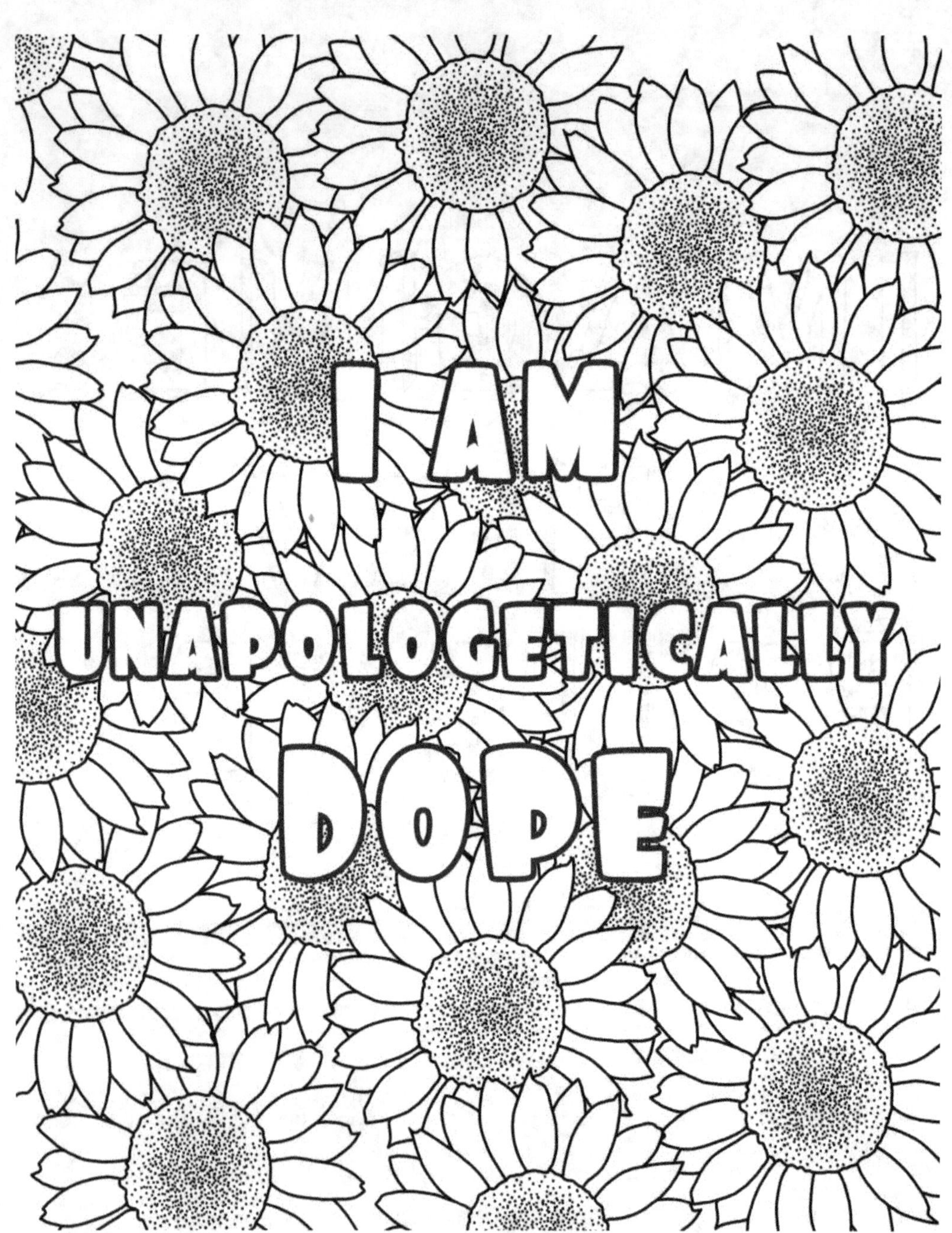
I AM
UNAPOLOGETICALLY
DOPE

www.unstoppablebylyn.com
Unapologetically Dope
PeriodT.

www.ingramcontent.com/pod-product-compliance
Lightning Source LLC
LaVergne TN
LVHW061226100826
845148LV00004B/877

* 9 7 8 1 7 3 4 5 0 9 9 3 9 *